ADVANCE PRAISE FOR *RECORD-BREAKING NATURAL DISASTERS*

"I thought this was a recipe book. It is not. I must have grabbed it by accident. I brought it home and read it to my grandson, but mid-sentence I realized that I don't have a grandson and was reading the book to a nearby pigeon in Central Park. The pigeon loved it. Five stars."
   —Genevieve Cosgrove, New York

"Coooo! Cooooooooo! Coo!"
   —That Pigeon in Central Park, New York

"This book washed ashore on an island I've been stranded on since 1997. Rather than reading it, I used a few pages to start a fire. I then painted a face on the back cover and named the book Kikoo. Kikoo and I have since been rescued and now rent a small apartment together in Seattle."
   —Tom H., Seattle

"Delicious!"
   —Paper Shredder, Texas

"The only thing better than this book is the creation of modern medicine, air-conditioning, and the everything bagel."
   —Definitely Not Mr. DeMaio, New Jersey . . . I mean, Spain . . . or something

4

PRESENTS!

RECORD-BREAKING NATURAL DISASTERS

by **Mr. DeMaio**

illustrated by **Saxton Moore**

GROSSET & DUNLAP

TABLE OF CONTENTS

② TABLE OF TABLES

EARTHQUAKES AND TSUNAMIS

EARTHQUAKE:

An earthquake is the result of a sudden release of stored energy in the Earth's crust that creates seismic waves.

TSUNAMI:

A series of long, high sea waves caused by an earthquake, landslide, meteor crash, or other disturbance.

RATING:

Richter Scale: Earthquakes are measured by something called the Richter scale. This scale measures earthquakes on a scale of 1.0 to 9.0 and higher. The higher the number, the stronger the earthquake.

VALDIVIA EARTHQUAKE
THE MOST POWERFUL EARTHQUAKE

WHAT TYPE OF NATURAL DISASTER: Earthquake

WHEN: May 22, 1960

WHERE: Chile, South America

SIZE: 9.4–9.6 magnitude

TOTAL DAMAGE: $400–$800 million

TOTAL CASUALTIES: 1,655

This earthquake caused a tsunami with waves that reached 6,000 miles away!

This quake created a fault line over 600 miles long! That's farther than the distance between New York City and Cincinnati!

600 MILES

40% of the houses in Valdivia were destroyed.

Scientists estimate that this earthquake shifted Earth's axis and shortened the length of a day by 1.26 microseconds.

LOOK! THE EARTH'S CRACK IS SHOWING.

SHAANXI EARTHQUAKE
THE DEADLIEST EARTHQUAKE

WHAT TYPE OF NATURAL DISASTER: Earthquake

WHEN: January 23, 1556

WHERE: Shaanxi, China

SIZE: 8.0 magnitude

TOTAL DAMAGE: The total cost in damages is unknown, but experts believe that it would be equal to an earthquake destroying as much land as New York, New Jersey, Pennsylvania, Delaware, Maryland, Washington, DC, Virginia, and West Virginia combined!

TOTAL CASUALTIES: 830,000

Ninety-seven counties were affected by this disaster.

HEY, GUYS! WHAT'S A MAGNET DUDE?

This earthquake destroyed a 520-mile-wide area in China.

The quake took the lives of 60% of the people living in Shaanxi and its neighboring province.

RANDOM QUESTION. WHAT DO YOU THINK THEY CALL EARTHquakes ON MARS?

INDIAN OCEAN EARTHQUAKE

THE LONGEST EARTHQUAKE AND DEADLIEST TSUNAMI

WHAT TYPE OF NATURAL DISASTER: Earthquake and Tsunami

WHEN: December 26, 2004

WHERE: Sumatra, Indonesia

SIZE: 9.1–9.3 magnitude

TOTAL DAMAGE: $15 billion

TOTAL CASUALTIES: 230,000

This earthquake lasted nearly 10 minutes and created 100-foot-high waves.

The energy from this quake is equivalent to over 1,500 times that of the atomic bomb dropped on Hiroshima.

INDIAN OCEAN EARTHQUAKE =
1,500 ✕

The shift of mass and the massive release of energy slightly altered the Earth's rotation. The exact amount is not yet known, but theoretical models suggest the earthquake shortened the length of a day by 2.68 microseconds.

Waves from the tsunami spread as far as South Africa, killing over 300 more people.

LITUYA BAY TSUNAMI
THE HIGHEST TSUNAMI

WHAT TYPE OF NATURAL DISASTER: Earthquake and Megatsunami

WHEN: July 9, 1958

WHERE: Lituya Bay, Alaska

CAUSE: This earthquake loosened nearly 40 million cubic yards of rock that fell 3,000 feet into Lituya Bay, hitting a giant glacier before falling into the water. The impact created a giant tsunami that crashed against the shore.

SIZE: 7.7–8.3 magnitude

WAVE HEIGHT: 1,720 feet!

SPEED: 90–130 mph

TOTAL DAMAGE: Unknown

TOTAL CASUALTIES: 5

LOOK, WAVE!

I CAN'T WAVE. I DON'T HAVE ANY HANDS!

The suggested wave height of 1,720 feet is taller than the Empire State Building in New York City.

WHAT AN EASY WORD SEARCH! ALL THE WORDS ARE IN ORDER. RIGHT, MONSIEUR FROG?

The native Tlingit people once spoke of a mysterious cave deep below Lituya Bay. In the cave lives the evil spirit *qa htu 'a* (say: KAN-li-tuya), similar in appearance to a great toad or frog. If someone dares to disturb its sleep, it will violently shake the land and the sea.

Even though this tsunami was extremely massive, it caused very little damage, only sinking one boat!

VOLCANOES

VOLCANO:

A rupture in the Earth's crust that causes molten lava, ash, and various gases to escape into the air from below the Earth's crust.

TYPES OF VOLCANOES:

CINDER CONES: The most simple and common type of volcano. They are circular or oval cones made up of a single vent.

STRATOVOLCANOES: These are volcanoes with steep sides that are comprised of many layers of volcanic rocks, usually made from thick lava, ash, and rock debris.

SHIELDS: These volcanoes are huge, gently sloping, and shaped like a bowl due to a very thin layer of lava spreading in all directions from one central vent.

LAVA DOMES: These are formed from lava that erupts but is too thick to flow and makes a steep-sided mound as the lava piles up near the volcanic vent.

RATING:

Volcanic Explosivity Index (VEI): VEI is the way to measure the explosiveness of a volcano. Volcanoes are measured on a scale of 0 to 8 by how much volcanic material is thrown out, the height of the material expelled, and how long the eruption lasts.

KRAKATOA
THE LOUDEST VOLCANIC ERUPTION

WHAT TYPE OF NATURAL DISASTER: Volcanic Eruption

TYPE OF VOLCANO: Stratovolcano

CURRENT ACTIVITY: Active

WHEN: August 26, 1883

WHERE: Krakatoa, Indonesia

RATING (VEI): 6

TOTAL DAMAGE: Unknown

TOTAL CASUALTIES: At least 35,000

The explosion could be heard nearly 3,000 miles away! That's farther than the distance between New York City and Los Angeles. It was louder than an atomic bomb explosion. Anyone within 10 miles of the eruption likely went deaf!

Only 66% of the island of Krakatoa remained after the explosion.

There was so much volcanic debris in the atmosphere that it changed the planet's temperature, making it nearly 2°F colder the following year.

A new volcano exists there today. Anak Krakatoa, meaning Child of Krakatoa, has emerged in the crater of the original Krakatoa and is still active today.

MOUNT TAMBORA
THE DEADLIEST VOLCANIC ERUPTION

WHAT TYPE OF NATURAL DISASTER: Volcanic Eruption

TYPE OF VOLCANO: Stratovolcano

CURRENT ACTIVITY: Active

WHEN: 1815

WHERE: Sumbawa, Indonesia

STRENGTH (VEI): 7

TOTAL DAMAGE: Unknown

TOTAL CASUALTIES: Estimated 10,000 local deaths and nearly 80,000 deaths caused from resulting starvation and disease

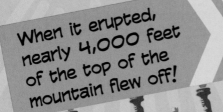

When it erupted, nearly 4,000 feet of the top of the mountain flew off!

Caused the "year without a summer" in 1816 when the planet's temperature dropped 5.4°F!

Plumes reached as high as twenty-five miles! That's higher than more than 400 Statues of Liberty!

I HOPE IT IS A WEIRD BROWN BALL WITH GLASSES!

KILAUEA
THE MOST ACTIVE VOLCANO

WHAT TYPE OF NATURAL DISASTER: Volcanic Eruption

TYPE OF VOLCANO: Shield

CURRENT ACTIVITY: Active . . . very active

WHEN: 1983-2018

WHERE: Hawaii, United States

STRENGTH (VEI): 3

TOTAL DAMAGE: $1-$20 million

TOTAL CASUALTIES: None

Despite volcanoes being incredibly dangerous, Kilauea has a golf course nearby that people played on amid the eruptions.

The volcano is believed to be between 210,000 and 280,000 years old and erupted almost continuously from 1983 to 2018.

It has had sixty-one different eruptions since 1823.

IS IT HOT IN HERE? OR IS THE EARTH SPEWING LIQUIDY DEATH FIRE WITHIN INCHES OF US?

SURT: IO SUPERVOLCANO
THE LARGEST ALIEN ERUPTION

WHAT TYPE OF NATURAL DISASTER: Volcano

WHEN: 2001

WHERE: Io (Moon of Jupiter)

STRENGTH (VEI): Unknown

TOTAL DAMAGE: None

TOTAL CASUALTIES: None

This volcano has such massive eruptions that we can see them with telescopes from Earth!

MAN, I FEEL BAD FOR WHOEVER HAS TO WEAR THAT OUTFIT NEXT.

It is believed that this volcano's plumes measure higher than 300 miles above the surface of Io. That's fifty-five times higher than Mount Everest!

The moon Io is covered in volcanoes, over 400 to be exact.

IO IS THE LAND OF FIRE AND ICE. EVEN THOUGH IT HAS INCREDIBLY HOT VOLCANOES THAT CAN REACH OVER 3,000°F, ITS SURFACE CAN REACH TEMPERATURES AS LOW AS -202°F!

During the 2001 explosion, scientists witnessed an eruption with an estimated energy output that is about 250 times stronger than the explosion of Krakatoa.

TORNADOES

TORNADO:

A violent destructive whirling wind that is accompanied by a funnel-shaped cloud that progresses in a narrow path over land.

RATING:

Enhanced Fujita Scale (EF Scale): Tornadoes are measured on the EF Scale. This scale measures the intensity of a tornado on a scale of 1 to 5.

FAJITAS?!?

STOP Holding this sign!

CHEFS MUST LOVE TO SERVE FAJITAS. THEY'RE LIKE, "HERE'S ALL THE INGREDIENTS! NOW MAKE IT YOURSELF!"

JOPLIN TORNADO
THE MOST DESTRUCTIVE TORNADO

WHAT TYPE OF NATURAL DISASTER: Tornado

WHEN: May 22, 2011

WHERE: Joplin, Missouri

WIND SPEED: 250 mph

RATING (EF SCALE): 5

TOTAL DAMAGE: $2.8 billion

TOTAL CASUALTIES: 158

About 9,200 people were displaced from their homes.

I MILE

The width of the tornado was one mile!

The tornado lasted thirty-eight minutes.

Its path was over twenty-two miles long, destroying anything in its way.

DON'T WORRY, GUYS. I'M A BROWN BELT! I'LL PROTECT YOU IF THAT TORNADO COMES NEAR US.

IF THAT TORNADO COMES NEAR US, I'M GOING TO HAVE MORE THAN A BROWN BELT!

DAULTIPUR-SATURIA TORNADO
THE DEADLIEST TORNADO

WHAT TYPE OF NATURAL DISASTER: Tornado

WHEN: April 26, 1989

WHERE: Manikganj District, Bangladesh

WIND SPEED: >200 mph

RATING (EF SCALE): 5

TOTAL DAMAGE: Around $1.5 million

TOTAL CASUALTIES: Estimated 1,300 fatalities, 12,000 injuries

The country of Bangladesh is ranked third in terms of tornado frequency.

Almost every home in the path of the tornado was completely destroyed.

THAT'S NOT A FOOD TRUCK!

EVERY TRUCK'S A FOOD TRUCK IF YOU'RE HUNGRY ENOUGH.

The width of this tornado was described as around one mile wide

It had a path that was about fifty miles long!

EL RENO TORNADO
THE BIGGEST TORNADO

WHAT TYPE OF NATURAL DISASTER: Tornado

WHEN: May 31, 2013

WHERE: El Reno, Oklahoma

WIND SPEED: >295 mph

RATING (EF SCALE): 5

TOTAL DAMAGE: $35–$40 million

TOTAL CASUALTIES: 13

This tornado lasted for forty minutes, causing millions of dollars in damages.

DO YOU THINK IF WE CHANGE IT FROM TORNADOES TO TORNADOESN'T, IT WILL STOP BEING SO WINDY?

NO . . . I DON'T THINK THAT WILL WORK AT ALL.

The width of the tornado was 2.6 miles. That's equivalent to the entire north to south length of New York City's Central Park.

2.6 MILES

2011 SUPER OUTBREAK
THE BIGGEST TORNADO OUTBREAK

WHAT TYPE OF NATURAL DISASTER: Tornado Outbreak

WHEN: April 25–28, 2011

WHERE: Alabama, Mississippi, Arkansas, Georgia, Tennessee, Virginia, Louisiana, Kentucky, Illinois, Ohio, Texas, and Oklahoma

WIND SPEED: >200 mph

RATING (EF SCALE): 5

TOTAL DAMAGE: $11 billion

TOTAL CASUALTIES: 324

It produced 360 tornadoes, with 60% of them occurring in a single 24-hour period. This outbreak of tornadoes lasted for longer than three days!

Alabama was hit the hardest, with sixty-two violent tornadoes touching down there.

x62

JEEZ! HOW DOES THAT THING SPIN FOR SO LONG?

GUYS . . . I JUST THREW UP A 1916 BUFFALO NICKEL.

THIS BOOK?!?!?
OR AN OKAY SOUP BOWL!
Okay, I know I don't usually wear pants, but if I did, they would be wet.
My paper cuts have paper cuts!
A NEW OUTFIT!
ALL FOR THE LOW PRICE OF . . . WHATEVER YOU PAID FOR THIS BOOK.

TROPICAL STORMS
HURRICANES, TYPHOONS, AND CYCLONES

ARCTIC
OCEAN

PACIFIC
OCEAN

TROPICAL STORM:

A tropical storm, also called typhoon, cyclone,
or hurricane, depending on where they form,
is an intense circular storm that begins over
warm tropical oceans and is characterized by
low atmospheric pressure, high winds,
and heavy rain.

RATING:

The Saffir-Simpson Hurricane Wind
Scale is a 1 to 5 rating based on a
hurricane's sustained wind speed and
the estimated property damage.

HURRICANE JOHN

THE LONGEST LASTING AND FARTHEST TRAVELED TROPICAL STORM

WHAT TYPE OF NATURAL DISASTER: Hurricane and Typhoon

WHEN: August 11–September 10, 1994

WHERE: Eastern and western Pacific Ocean

RATING: Category 5

SIZE: 930 miles wide

TOTAL DAMAGE: $15 million

TOTAL CASUALTIES: None

This massive storm lasted 31 days and traveled a path nearly 8,200 miles long.

8,200 MILES

Tropical storms in the eastern Pacific Ocean are called hurricanes, while tropical storms in the western Pacific are called typhoons. Hurricane John is both a hurricane *and* a typhoon because it traveled through both parts of the Pacific Ocean.

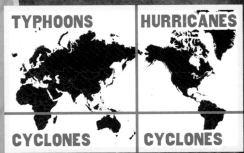

GUYS! YOU ARE NOT GOING TO BELIEVE WHAT'S OVER HERE!!!

GET . . . BACK . . . OVER . . . HERE . . .

It had wind speeds up to 175 mph. That's nearly as fast as a Ford Mustang.

BHOLA CYCLONE
THE DEADLIEST TROPICAL STORM

IT'S A GIANT CLOUD SHAPED LIKE A DOUGHNUT!

HOW DID WE EVEN GET TO THIS PAGE?

WHAT TYPE OF NATURAL DISASTER: Cyclone

WHEN: November 3–13, 1970

WHERE: India and Pakistan

RATING: Category 3

SIZE: 168 miles wide

TOTAL DAMAGE: Nearly $87 million

TOTAL CASUALTIES: 300,000 to 500,000

Its winds reached speeds up to 150 mph.

Waters in the area rose to thirty-five feet, causing massive flooding, which led to the majority of the deaths.

Approximately 85% of homes in the area were destroyed or severely damaged.

SOME GUY NAMED SAXTON MOORE IS DRAWING US. JUST LOOK WHAT HE DID TO JUSTIN.

WHERE ARE MY PANTS?

TYPHOON TIP

THE LARGEST AND MOST INTENSE TROPICAL STORM

WHAT TYPE OF NATURAL DISASTER: Typhoon

WHEN: October 4–24, 1979

WHERE: Northwest Pacific Ocean

RATING: Category 5

SIZE: 1,380 miles wide!

TOTAL DAMAGE: Unknown

TOTAL CASUALTIES: 99

The storm's huge width was nearly the same as the distance from New York City to Dallas.

It had wind speeds as high as 190 mph.

The storm lasted three weeks!

Although it weakened by the time it touched land, extensive flooding destroyed more than 20,000 homes in Japan.

WOW! COOL DOG!

WHY DO THEY CALL THESE THINGS HURRYCANES? THEY SHOULD CALL THEM "LASTS-A-FEW-WEEKS-A-CANES!"

THE GREAT RED SPOT

THE BIGGEST STORM IN OUR SOLAR SYSTEM

Gigantoor Alien Death Circle 9: Electric Boogaloo

WHAT TYPE OF NATURAL DISASTER: Anticyclonic Storm

WHEN: It's been observed on Jupiter ever since people started looking through telescopes, about 400 years ago.

WHERE: Jupiter

RATING: Category 1 Bazillion

SIZE: 10,160 miles wide

TOTAL DAMAGE: None

TOTAL CASUALTIES: None

That's seven times bigger than Typhoon Tip!

Jupiter's Great Red Spot is more than twice the size of Earth and has winds that can reach speeds over 400 mph!

Even though this storm is massive, it is currently shrinking!

It's not exactly a tropical storm. Tropical storms form over water. They are low-pressure systems where air is forced up through the center of the storm and directed toward the sky. An anticyclone is the opposite. It's a high-pressure system where air is forced downward through the center of the storm and toward the surface of the planet.

FLOODS AND WILDFIRES AND BLIZZARDS. OH MY!

FLOOD:

An overflow of water that submerges land.

WILDFIRE:

A large, destructive fire that spreads quickly over an area of land.

BLIZZARD:

An extreme snowstorm with high winds and low visibility.

I COULD REALLY GO FOR ONE OF THOSE WILDFIRES RIGHT ABOUT NOW . . .

1931 CHINA FLOODS
THE DEADLIEST FLOOD

WHAT TYPE OF NATURAL DISASTER: Flood

WHEN: April–November 1931

WHERE: Eastern and central China

CAUSE: Before the flood, China had some weird weather. They would have very little rain and then massive amounts of rain and snow! This added a ton of water to their rivers. Next, China was hit by many strong cyclones. Dykes and dams meant to control the rivers were built incorrectly, so when the crazy weather in 1931 happened, the rivers overflowed and water rushed across eastern and central China.

LAND DESTROYED: Over 23 million acres

TOTAL DAMAGE: Unknown

TOTAL CASUALTIES: Up to 4,000,000

Although many drowned in this flood, millions died from starvation and disease, even after the flood waters had receded.

THAT'S A LOT OF FEET!

53 FEET!

The highest levels of water recorded during the flood of 1931 was nearly fifty-three feet.

BLACK SUMMER (AUSTRALIAN WILDFIRES)

THE BIGGEST AND MOST DESTRUCTIVE WILDFIRE

WHAT TYPE OF NATURAL DISASTER: Wildfire

WHEN: June 2019–March 2020

WHERE: Australia

CAUSE: Australia has always experienced bushfires. It even has a "fire season." But in the year 2019, these fires were worse than usual. Higher than normal temperatures came on top of a long period of drought. Scientists have long warned that this hotter, drier climate will contribute to fires becoming more frequent and more intense. This is the leading theory on what caused the fires.

LAND DESTROYED: >40 million acres

TOTAL DAMAGE: Estimated $110 billion

TOTAL CASUALTIES: 34

An estimated 1.25 billion animals have been lost to the fires.

NOT ON OUR WATCH!

YOU GUYS GOT WATCHES? ALL I GOT WAS . . . EVERY ANIMAL SPECIES IN AUSTRALIA!

The wildfires covered an area larger than Portugal.

PESHTIGO FIRE
THE DEADLIEST WILDFIRE

WHAT TYPE OF NATURAL DISASTER: Wildfire

WHEN: October 8, 1871

WHERE: Peshtigo, Wisconsin

CAUSE: The fire is thought to have been caused by small fires used for land-clearing that blew out of control and created a firestorm.

LAND DESTROYED: Over 1 million acres

TOTAL DAMAGE: Estimated $169 million

TOTAL CASUALTIES: Estimated 2,500

There were many who believed that this fire—and the Great Chicago Fire—were caused by fragments of Biela's comet.

INTERESTING. I HAD NO IDEA FIRE WAS BLACK-AND-WHITE BACK THEN!

This fire occurred at the same time as the Great Chicago Fire but is not nearly as well known. Part of the reason it isn't as well known is because the telegraph lines in the area burned down so it took days before word spread about the fire.

The fire also burned sixteen other towns, but the damage in Peshtigo was the worst. The city was gone in an hour.

IRAN BLIZZARD
THE DEADLIEST BLIZZARD

WHAT TYPE OF NATURAL DISASTER: Blizzard

WHEN: February 3-9, 1972

WHERE: Iran

AMOUNT OF SNOW: 26 feet! That's taller than a giraffe!

TOTAL DAMAGE: Unknown

TOTAL CASUALTIES: 4,000

About 6,000 people went missing at the time of the blizzard.

× 6,000

HOW ARE GIRAFFES REAL BUT UNICORNS AREN'T?

STORM OF THE CENTURY
THE MOST DESTRUCTIVE BLIZZARD

WHAT TYPE OF NATURAL DISASTER: Tornado and Blizzard

WHEN: March 12–14, 1993

WHERE: North America

AMOUNT OF SNOW: 1 to 6 feet of snow all across the eastern United States

TOTAL DAMAGE: $5.5 billion

TOTAL CASUALTIES: 318

The storm covered more than 550,000 square miles.

In addition to the snow, an estimated fifteen tornadoes struck Florida.

TORNADO X 15 EQUALS . . . 64!

Some snow drifts were as high as thirty-five feet.

AVALANCHES AND LANDSLIDES

AVALANCHE:

A giant mass of snow, ice, and rocks that falls rapidly down a mountainside.

LANDSLIDE:

A giant mass of rocks and dirt that falls rapidly down a cliff or mountainside.

I SHALL NAME YOU DIRT REYNOLDS.

ANCASH AVALANCHE
THE BIGGEST AND DEADLIEST AVALANCHE

WHAT TYPE OF NATURAL DISASTER: Avalanche

WHEN: May 31, 1970

WHERE: Peru

CAUSE: Earthquake

TOTAL DAMAGE: Unknown

TOTAL CASUALTIES: About 70,000

The avalanche started as a sliding mass of glacial ice and rock about 3,000 feet wide and one mile long. That's more than two times the size of Disneyland.

The giant ice slid down the side of a mountain at an average speed of more than 100 miles an hour.

SPEED LIMIT 100

WHOA! ARE WE GOING TO MELT THE SNOW IF AN AVALANCHE COMES?

NO . . . I JUST THOUGHT THIS WOULD LOOK COOL.

DON'T TRY THIS AT HOME . . . OR IN AN AVALANCHE.

AGULHAS SLIDE
THE LARGEST SUBMARINE LANDSLIDE

WHAT TYPE OF NATURAL DISASTER: Underwater Landslide

WHEN: 2.6 million years ago

WHERE: South Africa

CAUSE: Unknown

TOTAL DAMAGE: Unknown

TOTAL CASUALTIES: Unknown

MAN, HOW DID THIS UNKNOWN GUY LIVE THROUGH SO MANY NATURAL DISASTERS?!? I WONDER WHAT HIS SECRET IS . . .

I BET YOU HE CUT OUT GLUTEN.

This landslide displaced what is equal to 5,283,441,047,162,968 gallons of landmass. That's nearly enough to fill *all* of the Great Lakes.

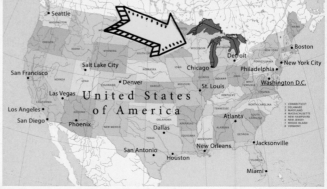

This event occurred right around the time the megalodon went extinct!
WHOA! THE MEGALODON! I SURE WISH I COULD SEE ONE OF THOSE IN MY LIFETIME!
YEAH! ME TOO! IF ONLY THERE WAS ONE WE COULD SEE . . .

HAIYUAN LANDSLIDE
THE DEADLIEST LANDSLIDE

WHAT TYPE OF NATURAL DISASTER: Earthquake and Landslide

WHEN: December 16, 1920

WHERE: Haiyuan County, China

CAUSE: Earthquake

TOTAL DAMAGE: Unknown

TOTAL CASUALTIES: 70,000–200,000 (including from the earthquake)

The earthquake generated a series of 675 landslides, causing massive destruction to lives and property.

These landslides destroyed over 70,000 square miles of land. That's as big as North Dakota!

HURRY UP! LANDSLIDES ARE DANGEROUS.

RELAX! LANDSLIDE IS MY MIDDLE NAME. ACTUALLY, MY MIDDLE NAME IS DENNIS, BUT YOU GET THE POINT.

Landslides can reach speeds up to thirty-five mph! That's about seven mph faster than the fastest man who has ever lived!

ER . . .

Did you know male ladybugs are just called ladybugs?

Zebras are not spicy horses. Although they do belong to the same family of mammals as horses, called equids, they are one of several horse-like African mammals; each species has a characteristic pattern of black or dark brown stripes on a whitish background.

The lamp you would see in movies featuring genies is not an actual electric lamp. It's actually an oil lamp!

ACKNOWLEDGMENTS

MOM & DAD

You are the source of my imagination and my kindness. Thanks for letting me watch all those crazy movies and TV shows as a kid, for our many vacations to that mouse-themed place that I cannot name due to copyright reasons, for allowing me to draw and create things endlessly, and for encouraging me to have the imagination I have today. You fostered the creativity that got me where I am.

NICK MAGLIATO

Thank you for plucking me out of the world and giving me this opportunity. All I've ever wanted to do was make a difference in the world. Without your help, I'm not sure I would have ever been able to do that. I owe ya!

EMILY

For years you have tolerated my corny jokes, weird impersonations, puppets being thrown about our house, green screens hanging in our kitchen, and more. Where most would have lost their mind, you encouraged me to carry on. I am a lucky guy and I love you.

DENNIS

I am forever grateful for your help and guidance. You are a great friend.

STUDENTS OF MEMORIAL SCHOOL

This all started with you. YOU all pushed me to create videos. YOU inspired me to be creative and think outside the box. Whenever I thought I would quit, the thought of your laughing faces pushed me to create more and more. Usually, it is the teacher that inspires the students but in this case, you inspired me. For that, I dedicate this book to all of you.

GROSSET & DUNLAP
An Imprint of Penguin Random House LLC, New York

Illustrations by Saxton Moore
Author photo by Emily DeMaio
All other images credited to Getty Images

Visit us online at www.penguinrandomhouse.com.

Library of Congress Cataloging-in-Publication Data
is available upon request.

ISBN 9780593224786   10 9 8 7 6 5 4 3 2 1 TC